The Anxiety-Free Zone

A Step-by-Step Guide to Managing Anxiety and Stress for Good

Dr. Melinda Hope

Table of Contents

Introduction

Welcome to "The Anxiety-Free Zone: A Step-by-Step Guide to Managing Anxiety and Stress for Good." If you're holding this book, chances are you've experienced the weight of anxiety and the relentless grip of stress. Take a deep breath, you're not alone. We, too, have navigated the labyrinth of worry, uncertainty, and sleepless nights. This book isn't just a guide; it's a companion on your journey toward a life free from the suffocating clutches of anxiety.

Picture this: a life where every breath isn't a struggle, where your mind isn't a battlefield, and where stress doesn't dictate your every move. It's not a distant dream; it's an achievable reality, and we're here to walk this path with you.

I know the knots in your stomach, the racing heartbeat that echoes your deepest fears. Anxiety isn't just a word; it's a symphony of emotions that can be all-consuming. I've been there, the sleepless nights, the moments of panic that feel like an eternity. But I also know the transformative power of resilience, the strength we find in vulnerability, and the beauty of reclaiming control over our minds.

In these pages, we'll unravel the layers of anxiety together, peeling back the heavy cloak that shrouds your potential for joy. I won't promise an overnight miracle, conquering anxiety is a journey, not a sprint. But what I can promise is that with each turn of the page, you'll discover tools, insights, and stories that resonate with your struggles.

This book is more than just advice; it's a collection of shared experiences, a testament to the human spirit's ability to triumph over adversity. We'll explore the science behind stress, delve into practical coping mechanisms, and carve out a personalized roadmap to your anxiety-free zone.

So, let's embark on this journey hand in hand. We're not just authors; we're fellow travelers who believe in your strength, your resilience, and your capacity for change. It's time to transform your anxious today into a peaceful tomorrow. Turn the page, and let the journey begin.

Chapter 1

Unmasking Anxiety

Identifying Different Forms of Anxiety

Anxiety is more than a passing worry; it's a spectrum of emotions that can range from mild unease to debilitating fear.

Tip: Notice physical symptoms like restlessness, tense muscles, or rapid heartbeat as potential signs of anxiety.

Types of Anxiety Disorders

1. Generalized Anxiety Disorder (GAD)
Persistent, excessive worry about various aspects of life.
Example: Worrying about work, health, family, and more, even when there's no apparent reason.

2. Social Anxiety Disorder

Intense fear of social situations, often leading to avoidance.

Example: Feeling anxious in social gatherings, fearing judgment or scrutiny.

3. Panic Disorder

Sudden, intense episodes of fear accompanied by physical symptoms.

Example: Unexpected panic attacks, sometimes mistaken for a heart attack.

4. Obsessive-Compulsive Disorder (OCD)

Intrusive thoughts (obsessions) leading to repetitive behaviors (compulsions).

Example: Constantly checking things or repeating specific actions.

5. Post-Traumatic Stress Disorder (PTSD)

Anxiety triggered by past traumatic events.

Example: Flashbacks, nightmares, or severe anxiety related to a traumatic experience.

The Unseen Struggles

Highlight: Anxiety isn't always obvious. It can manifest as chronic stress, phobias, or subtle behavioral changes.

Prompt: Reflect on moments when stress or worry impacted your daily life.

Real-world Example

Case Study: Emily's Story

Emily struggled with constant worry about her performance at work, leading to sleepless nights and difficulty concentrating.

Connection: Many can relate to the pressure of work-related stress.

Call-to-Action

1. **Self-Reflection:** Identify one situation where anxiety has affected your daily life.

2. **Journaling:** Write down your feelings during anxious moments, noting triggers and physical sensations.

3. **Reach Out:** Share your experiences with a trusted friend or family member to begin breaking the stigma around anxiety.

Recognizing Triggers

Unveiling the Catalysts

Triggers Defined: Triggers are events, thoughts, or situations that set off anxiety or stress. Identifying them is key to effective management.

Common Triggers

1. Stressful Situations

Example: Tight deadlines, conflict, or major life changes.

Tip: Notice patterns, do specific situations consistently heighten your anxiety?

2. Negative Thinking Patterns

Example: Catastrophizing (expecting the worst), overgeneralizing, or black-and-white thinking.

Spotting It: Pay attention to your thought patterns during stressful moments.

3. Physical Factors

Example: Lack of sleep, poor nutrition, or caffeine intake.

Connection: Physical well-being directly impacts mental health.

4. Environmental Triggers

Example: Crowded places, noise, or specific locations tied to past stress.

Action: Be aware of environments that contribute to unease.

Personal Triggers

Exercise: List personal triggers in your journal.

Example: Public speaking, financial discussions, or uncertainty about the future.

Insight: Understanding personal triggers is crucial for tailored anxiety management.

The Power of Awareness

Bold Move: Acknowledging triggers isn't a sign of weakness; it's a strength.

Reminder: Identifying triggers doesn't mean avoiding them but learning to navigate through them.

Real-world Example

Case Study: Jake's Challenge

Jake realized his anxiety spiked during team meetings at work.

Solution: Understanding the trigger allowed Jake to implement pre-meeting calming exercises.

Call-to-Action

1. **Trigger Log:** Create a simple log noting situations triggering anxiety.
2. **Mindful Observation:** Observe your thoughts and emotions during a trigger without judgment.
3. **Seek Patterns:** Identify recurring triggers to enhance self-awareness.

Recognizing triggers is a pivotal step toward gaining control over anxiety. As we move forward, we'll explore practical techniques to cope with these triggers effectively.

Chapter 2

The Science of Stress

How Stress Affects the Body and Mind

Understanding the Stress Response

Introduction: Stress is more than an emotion; it's a physiological response hardwired into our biology.
Key Point: The body's "fight or flight" response is a primal reaction to perceived threats.

The Body's Stress Arsenal

1. Release of Stress Hormones
Culprits: Cortisol and adrenaline surge to prepare the body for action.
Effect: Heightened alertness, increased heart rate, and redirected energy.

2. Impact on Immune System

Connection: Chronic stress weakens the immune system.

Example: Frequent illnesses or prolonged recovery from illnesses.

3. Digestive System Response

Effect: Blood flow shifts from digestion to essential functions.

Result: Digestive issues, nausea, or changes in appetite.

Cognitive Impact

Memory and Focus: Stress impairs short-term memory and narrows the focus to immediate threats.

Connection to Anxiety: Chronic stress is a precursor to anxiety disorders.

Breaking It Down: The Stress Cycle

Diagram: Visual representation of the stress cycle from trigger to response.

Narrative: Understand the cyclical nature of stress to disrupt it effectively.

Real-world Example

Case Study: Sarah's Stress Spiral
Sarah experienced work-related stress, leading to insomnia and irritability.
Lesson: Recognizing stress patterns helped Sarah intervene early.

Call-to-Action

1. **Body Scan Meditation:** Practice a short body scan to identify physical stress indicators.
2. **Stress Journal:** Document stress triggers and physical/mental responses.
3. **Educate Yourself:** Read about the long-term effects of chronic stress for deeper understanding.

The Connection Between Anxiety and Stress

Unraveling the Intricate Link

Stress as the Precursor

Foundation: Understanding stress is crucial to comprehending its connection to anxiety.

Insight: Stress often lays the groundwork for anxiety to take root.

Chronic Stress and Anxiety

1. Impact on Brain Chemistry

Chemical Changes: Prolonged stress alters neurotransmitter levels.

Result: Increased susceptibility to anxiety disorders.

2. Worsening of Existing Anxiety

Example: Individuals with generalized anxiety may find their symptoms exacerbated by chronic stress.

Key Point: Stress acts as a catalyst for existing anxiety conditions.

The Feedback Loop

Visualization: Imagine stress and anxiety as interconnected loops feeding into each other.

Understanding the Loop: Stress contributes to anxiety, and heightened anxiety amplifies stress responses.

Physiological Responses

1. Shared Physical Symptoms

Overlap: Both stress and anxiety manifest in physical symptoms like tense muscles and rapid heartbeat.

Tip: Differentiating between the two helps in targeted management.

2. Impact on the Nervous System

Connection: Chronic stress activates the sympathetic nervous system.

Result: Constant arousal can evolve into anxiety disorders.

Real-world Example

Case Study: Alex's Journey

Alex's high-stress job led to persistent anxiety, affecting personal relationships.

Lesson: Recognizing the interplay allowed Alex to address both stress and anxiety.

Breaking the Chain

Mindfulness Practice: Techniques like meditation interrupt the stress-anxiety loop.
Cognitive Behavioral Therapy (CBT): Addressing negative thought patterns breaks the cycle.

Call-to-Action

1. **Journal Prompt:** Reflect on moments where stress escalated into anxiety.
2. **Mind-Body Exercise:** Engage in a stress-reducing activity (e.g., yoga) to observe its impact on anxiety.
3. **Professional Guidance:** Consider therapy to navigate and break the stress-anxiety cycle.

Understanding the connection between anxiety and stress is pivotal to effective management. As we progress, we'll explore strategies to break this connection and cultivate lasting calm.

Chapter 3

Building Your Foundation

Establishing a Positive Mindset

The Power of Mindset

Foundation: Your mindset is the bedrock of your emotional well-being.

Key Insight: Cultivating a positive mindset is a proactive step toward managing anxiety.

Embracing Positivity

1. Positive Affirmations

Technique: Repeat affirmations to challenge negative thoughts.

Example: "I am capable and resilient."

2. Gratitude Practice

Daily Ritual: List three things you're grateful for each day.

Effect: Shifts focus from stressors to positive aspects of life.

Self-Compassion

Reminder: Treat yourself with the same kindness you would a friend facing challenges.
Technique: Replace self-criticism with self-compassionate language.

Cognitive Restructuring

1. Identifying Negative Thoughts
Exercise: Journal negative thoughts as they arise.
Objective: Recognize patterns to challenge and reframe them.

2. Refocusing Techniques
Visualization: Imagine a stop sign when negative thoughts arise.
Affirmation Integration: Replace negative thoughts with positive affirmations.

Real-world Example

Case Study: Maria's Transformation
Maria shifted from self-doubt to confidence by integrating positive affirmations.
Lesson: Mindset shifts are gradual but impactful.

Building Resilience

Metaphor: Think of resilience as a muscle; it strengthens with practice.
Practice: Embrace challenges with a mindset focused on growth and learning.

Call-to-Action

1. **Positive Affirmation Creation:** Craft three personalized positive affirmations.
2. **Gratitude Journal:** Start a daily gratitude journal for the next week.
3. **Thought Awareness:** Practice recognizing and challenging negative thoughts.

By building a positive mindset, you're laying the groundwork for resilience in the face of anxiety. In the following chapters, we'll explore additional tools to fortify this foundation and navigate the complexities of stress and anxiety with newfound strength.

Setting Realistic Expectations

Navigating the Balance

The Pitfalls of Unrealistic Expectations

Insight: Unrealistic expectations can amplify stress and contribute to anxiety.

Common Traps: Perfectionism, overcommitment, and rigid goal-setting.

Embracing Realism

1. Defining Realistic Goals

Guideline: Goals should be challenging yet attainable.

Example: Instead of "perfection," aim for progress.

2. Understanding Limitations

Reality Check: Acknowledge your capacities and potential constraints.

Shift Perspective: It's okay not to excel in every aspect of life simultaneously.

The Art of Prioritization

Key Principle: Not everything is equally important or urgent.

Technique: Use the Eisenhower Matrix to categorize tasks by urgency and importance.

Time Management Strategies

1. Setting Boundaries

Example: Clearly communicate limits at work or in personal commitments.
Reminder: Boundaries are a form of self-care, not selfishness.

2. Allocating Breaks

Technique: Schedule short breaks during tasks to prevent burnout.
Result: Improved focus and sustained energy.

Real-world Example

Case Study: James' Journey
James reduced work-related stress by reassessing priorities and setting realistic deadlines.
Lesson: Small adjustments lead to significant stress reduction.

Cultivating Flexibility

Mindset Shift: Embrace flexibility as a strength, not a weakness.

Mantra: "I am adaptable and resilient in the face of change."

Call-to-Action

1. **Goal Reflection:** Evaluate one current goal—Is it realistic? Adjust if needed.
2. **Boundary Setting:** Identify one area where setting clear boundaries could alleviate stress.
3. **Flexibility Exercise:** Practice adapting to unexpected changes with a positive mindset.

By setting realistic expectations, you're creating a sustainable framework for success while mitigating the risk of overwhelming stress and anxiety. As we progress, we'll continue to explore practical strategies for maintaining balance in various aspects of life.

Chapter 4

Tools for Coping

Breathing Exercises

The Breath-Mind Connection

Fundamental Truth: Your breath is both a reflection and an influencer of your mental state.

Importance: Controlling your breath can directly impact stress and anxiety levels.

Deep Belly Breathing

1. Technique

Step 1: Inhale deeply through your nose, allowing your belly to expand.

Step 2: Exhale slowly through pursed lips, contracting your abdominal muscles.

Repeat: Practice for several minutes.

2. Benefits

Calming Effect: Activates the body's relaxation response.
Accessibility: This can be done anywhere, anytime.

Box Breathing

1. Technique
Step 1: Inhale for a count of four.
Step 2: Hold your breath for a count of four.
Step 3: Exhale for a count of four.
Step 4: Hold your breath for a count of four.
Repeat: Gradually increase the count as you become more comfortable.

2. Purpose
Focus and Clarity: Enhances mental focus and reduces stress.
Balancing Effect: Brings a sense of equilibrium.

4-7-8 Breathing

1. Technique
Step 1: Inhale quietly through your nose for a count of four.

Step 2: Hold your breath for a count of seven.

Step 3: Exhale completely through your mouth for a count of eight.

Repeat: Perform the cycle at least three times.

2. Stress Reduction

Relaxation Response: Activates the body's natural calming mechanisms.

Sleep Aid: Effective for promoting relaxation before bedtime.

Real-world Example

Case Study: Maya's Daily Practice

Incorporating deep belly breathing into her morning routine significantly reduced Maya's work-related stress.

Tip: Integrate breathing exercises into daily rituals for consistent benefits.

Creating a Breath Ritual

Reminder: Consistency is key for maximum impact.

Integration: Choose specific times to incorporate breathing exercises, such as morning routines or before stressful situations.

Call-to-Action

1. **Daily Breathing Ritual:** Allocate five minutes each day for deep belly breathing.
2. **Stressful Situation Breathing:** Practice box breathing the next time you encounter a stressful situation.
3. **Reflect and Adjust:** Notice the impact of these exercises and adjust your approach as needed.

As you embark on this journey of coping tools, remember that your breath is a powerful ally in managing stress and anxiety. In the next chapter, we'll explore mindfulness and meditation techniques to further enhance your coping toolkit.

Mindfulness and Meditation Techniques

The Transformative Power of Presence

Definition: Mindfulness is the practice of being fully present and engaged in the current moment.

Purpose: Cultivating mindfulness can significantly reduce stress and anxiety.

Mindfulness Meditation

1. Guided Practice

Step 1: Find a quiet space and sit comfortably.

Step 2: Focus on your breath, bringing your attention back when the mind wanders.

Step 3: Expand awareness to bodily sensations, sounds, and thoughts.

Duration: Start with 5-10 minutes, gradually increasing.

2. Benefits

Stress Reduction: Promotes a state of calm and relaxation.

Improved Focus: Enhances concentration and cognitive function.

Loving-Kindness Meditation

1. Guided Practice

Step 1: Begin by directing love and kindness towards yourself.

Step 2: Extend these feelings to loved ones, acquaintances, and even those you may have conflicts with.

Step 3: Broaden the scope to encompass all beings.

Duration: Adjust based on comfort, starting with 10-15 minutes.

2. Purpose

Cultivating Compassion: Foster's feelings of goodwill and compassion.

Positive Mindset: Shifts focus from negativity to kindness.

Body Scan Meditation

1. Guided Practice

Step 1: Lie down in a comfortable position.

Step 2: Mentally scan and release tension from each part of your body.

Step 3: Focus on the sensations in each area.

Duration: 15-20 minutes, adjusting as needed.

2. Physical Awareness

Stress Release: Promotes physical relaxation, reducing overall stress.

Mind-Body Connection: Strengthens awareness of the body's signals.

Real-world Example

Case Study: Tom's Mindfulness Journey
Incorporating mindfulness meditation into his routine helped Tom manage work-related stress.

Tip: Start with short sessions and gradually extend the duration as you become more comfortable.

Integration into Daily Life

Micro-Mindfulness: Infuse brief moments of mindfulness into everyday activities.

Example: Pause and take a few mindful breaths while waiting in line or during routine tasks.

Call-to-Action

1. **Daily Mindfulness Moment:** Set a daily reminder for a brief mindfulness break.

2. Loving-Kindness Exercise: Practice loving-kindness meditation for a loved one and extend it to others.

3. Body Scan Routine: Try a body scan meditation before bedtime for improved sleep.

As you explore these mindfulness and meditation techniques, remember that consistency is key to unlocking their full benefits. In the upcoming chapter, we'll delve into visualization practices to further enhance your stress management toolkit.

Visualization Practices

Harnessing the Power of Imagination

Introduction: Visualization involves creating vivid mental images to evoke a specific experience or outcome.

Purpose: Visualization can be a potent tool for reducing stress and promoting a positive mindset.

Guided Imagery

1. Setting the Scene

Step 1: Find a quiet space and get into a comfortable position.

Step 2: Close your eyes and envision a peaceful, serene place.

Step 3: Engage all your senses—feel the warmth, hear the sounds, and breathe in the scents.

2. Application

Stress Reduction: Transport yourself mentally to a calming environment during stressful moments.

Goal Achievement: Visualize successfully navigating challenges or achieving specific goals.

Future Self Visualization

1. Creating a Mental Image

Step 1: Imagine your ideal future self, thriving and content.

Step 2: Visualize the details—your surroundings, activities, and emotional state.

Step 3: Engage emotionally with this future version of yourself.

2. Benefits

Motivation: Cultivates a sense of purpose and direction.

Confidence Building: Boosts self-confidence by envisioning success.

Positive Outcome Visualization

1. Focus on a Goal

Step 1: Identify a specific goal or challenge.

Step 2: Envision the entire process, from preparation to successful completion.

Step 3: Picture the positive emotions associated with achievement.

2. Enhanced Performance

Preparation: Mentally prepares you for upcoming challenges.

Anxiety Reduction: Diminishes anxiety by familiarizing your mind with positive outcomes.

Real-world Example

Case Study: Lisa's Visualization Journey

Lisa used guided imagery to mentally rehearse job interviews, alleviating anxiety.

Tip: Practice visualization regularly for optimal results.

Integration into Daily Routine

Morning Visualization: Set a positive tone for the day with a brief visualization of a successful day.

Pre-Sleep Visualization: Calm the mind before bedtime by imagining a peaceful scenario.

Call-to-Action

1. **Guided Imagery Session:** Dedicate 10 minutes to a guided imagery session.

2. **Future Self Reflection:** Envision your future self in a moment of triumph or contentment.

3. Goal Visualization Exercise: Visualize achieving a specific goal, focusing on the journey and positive emotions.

Visualization practices are versatile tools that can be tailored to your specific needs. As we move forward, we'll explore lifestyle changes that support long-term stress management and anxiety relief.

Chapter 5

Lifestyle Changes for Long-Term Relief

Healthy Diet and Nutrition

The Mind-Body Connection

Foundation: The food you consume directly impacts your mental and emotional well-being.

Key Insight: A balanced, nutritious diet can be a cornerstone for managing stress and anxiety.

The Role of Nutrients

1. Omega-3 Fatty Acids

Source: Found in fatty fish, flaxseeds, and walnuts.

Benefits: Supports brain health, reducing symptoms of anxiety.

2. Complex Carbohydrates

Sources: Whole grains, fruits, and vegetables.

Effect: Stabilizes blood sugar levels, promoting consistent energy and mood.

3. Protein-Rich Foods
Sources: Lean meats, legumes, and dairy.
Importance: Aids in the production of neurotransmitters that regulate mood.

Hydration for Mental Clarity

Reminder: Dehydration can negatively impact cognitive function and exacerbate stress.
Tip: Ensure regular water intake throughout the day.

Mindful Eating Practices

1. Savoring Each Bite
Technique: Eat slowly, paying attention to taste, texture, and aroma.
Outcome: Enhances satisfaction and reduces overeating.

2. Balanced Meals
Recommendation: Include a mix of protein, healthy fats, and carbohydrates in each meal.
Effect: Promotes sustained energy and mood stability.

Real-world Example

Case Study: David's Nutritional Transformation
Adopting a diet rich in omega-3s and whole foods positively impacted David's overall mood.
Tip: Gradual changes to dietary habits can yield lasting benefits.

The Gut-Brain Connection

Insight: The gut microbiome influences mental health.
Recommendation: Incorporate probiotics and fiber-rich foods for a healthy gut.

Limiting Caffeine and Sugar

Caffeine Impact: Excessive caffeine can exacerbate feelings of anxiety and disrupt sleep.
Sugar Connection: High sugar intake may contribute to mood swings and energy crashes.

Call-to-Action

1. **Nutrient-Rich Meal:** Plan and prepare a meal with a balance of nutrients.

2. Hydration Challenge: Track your water intake for a week, ensuring you meet the recommended levels.

3. Mindful Eating Exercise: Dedicate one meal to mindful eating, savoring each bite.

Your dietary choices are potent tools for managing stress and anxiety. As we progress, we'll explore the equally vital aspects of regular exercise and adequate sleep in promoting long-term well-being.

Regular Exercise and Its Impact on Anxiety

Unleashing the Power of Physical Activity

Foundation: Regular exercise is not just beneficial for physical health but is a potent ally in managing mental well-being.

Key Point: Engaging in physical activity can significantly reduce symptoms of anxiety.

The Stress-Relief Mechanism

1. Endorphin Release

Effect: Exercise triggers the release of endorphins, the body's natural mood lifters.

Result: Enhanced feelings of well-being and reduced stress.

2. Stress Hormone Regulation

Cortisol Impact: Exercise helps regulate cortisol, the stress hormone.

Outcome: Improved stress response and resilience.

Choosing Your Exercise Regimen

1. Aerobic Exercise
Activities: Running, cycling, swimming.
Benefits: Boosts endorphins and improves cardiovascular health.

2. Strength Training
Activities: Weightlifting, resistance training.
Effect: Enhances overall physical and mental strength.

3. Mind-Body Exercises
Examples: Yoga, tai chi, Pilates.
Advantage: Combines physical activity with mindfulness, doubling stress-relief benefits.

Consistency is Key

Guideline: Aim for at least 150 minutes of moderate-intensity exercise per week.
Tip: Find activities you enjoy to increase the likelihood of long-term adherence.

Real-world Example

Case Study: Sarah's Exercise Routine

Regular jogging not only improved Sarah's physical fitness but also became a cornerstone in managing her anxiety.

Tip: Start with activities you enjoy; the key is consistency.

The Mindful Movement Approach

Connection: Combine exercise with mindfulness for a holistic approach.

Example: Pay attention to the sensations in your body during a jog or focus on your breath during yoga.

Outdoor Activities and Nature

Bonus Benefits: Exercising outdoors, especially in natural settings, amplifies the positive impact on mental well-being.

Tip: Incorporate outdoor activities like hiking, biking, or simply taking a walk in a nearby park.

Call-to-Action

1. **Physical Activity Exploration:** Try a new exercise or tten favorite.

2. Weekly Exercise Plan: Outline a manageable exercise routine for the upcoming week.

3. Mindful Movement Practice: Integrate mindfulness into your exercise routine, paying attention to the present moment.

Regular exercise is a dynamic component in your arsenal against anxiety. As we delve further into lifestyle changes, the next chapter will explore the critical role of adequate sleep in maintaining mental and emotional balance.

Adequate Sleep and Its Role in Stress Management

Unlocking the Healing Power of Sleep

Foundation: Quality sleep is an essential pillar for overall health, influencing both physical and mental well-being.

Key Insight: Insufficient sleep can exacerbate stress and anxiety.

The Sleep-Stress Connection

1. Impact on Stress Hormones

Cortisol Regulation: Adequate sleep supports a healthy cortisol rhythm.

Outcome: Improved stress response and resilience.

2. Emotional Regulation

REM Sleep: Vital for emotional processing and regulation.

Effect: Enhances emotional resilience and reduces reactivity to stressors.

Creating a Sleep-Positive Environment

1. Dark and Quiet Atmosphere

Tip: Use blackout curtains and consider white noise if needed.

Effect: Enhances melatonin production, a hormone crucial for sleep.

2. Comfortable Sleep Setting

Quality Mattress and Pillows: Invest in comfort for better sleep quality.

Temperature Control: Keep the bedroom cool for optimal sleep.

Establishing a Sleep Routine

1. Consistent Sleep Schedule

Importance: A regular sleep pattern regulates the body's internal clock.

Tip: Aim for consistent bedtime and wake-up times, even on weekends.

2. Wind-Down Routine

Activities: Read a book, and practice relaxation techniques.

Objective: Signal to the body that it's time to transition into sleep.

Real-world Example

Case Study: Mark's Sleep Transformation
Prioritizing a consistent sleep schedule and creating a calming bedtime routine significantly reduced Mark's overall stress levels.
Tip: Small adjustments to your sleep habits can yield significant improvements.

The Role of Naps

Strategic Napping: Short naps (20-30 minutes) can provide a quick energy boost without disrupting nighttime sleep.
Caution: Avoid long naps, especially in the late afternoon.

Mindfulness and Sleep

Technique: Use mindfulness or meditation practices to quiet the mind before bedtime.
Example: Focus on your breath or practice a body scan to relax.

Call-to-Action

1. Sleep Environment Evaluation: Assess your bedroom for factors influencing sleep quality.

2. Consistent Sleep Schedule: Commit to a consistent bedtime for the upcoming week.

3. Mindful Bedtime Routine: Integrate a brief mindfulness exercise into your wind-down routine.

Adequate sleep is a fundamental contributor to stress management. In the next chapter, we'll explore the importance of developing a support system and seeking professional help when needed.

Chapter 6

Developing a Support System

Communicating with Friends and Family

The Importance of Connection

Foundation: Building a strong support system is vital for emotional well-being and stress management.

Key Insight: Open communication with friends and family fosters understanding and provides a valuable network.

Opening Up About Stress and Anxiety

1. Choosing the Right Time

Tip: Select a calm and private setting for meaningful conversations.

Objective: Create an environment conducive to open dialogue.

2. Expressing Feelings Clearly

Use "I" Statements: Share your experiences without placing blame.

Example: "I've been feeling overwhelmed, and I could use your support."

Providing Information on Anxiety

Education: Offer basic information about anxiety to help loved ones understand the challenges you're facing.

Example: Share snippets from reputable sources or recommend resources for further reading.

Setting Boundaries and Expectations

1. Clearly Define Needs

Example: "I may need some alone time during high-stress periods, and I appreciate your understanding."

Outcome: Establishes clear expectations for support.

2. Boundaries for Self-Care

Tip: Emphasize the importance of self-care practices.

Example: "I'm working on incorporating stress-reducing activities, and I'd love your encouragement."

Real-world Example

Case Study: Emma's Candid Conversation
Emma opened up to her close friend about her anxiety, fostering a deeper understanding.
Lesson: Honest communication strengthens relationships.

Encouraging Active Listening

Role of the Listener: Actively listen without judgment or immediate problem-solving.
Response: Encourage open-ended questions and provide reassurance.

Seeking Professional Support Together

Encouragement: Suggest the idea of seeking professional help together.
Example: "I'm considering therapy, and having your support would mean a lot to me."

1. Select a Trusted Person: Choose one friend or family member to confide in about your feelings.

2. Plan the Conversation: Consider the optimal time and place for a heartfelt conversation.

3. Express Your Needs: Clearly communicate your needs and expectations for support.

Developing a support system begins with open communication. In the following chapter, we'll explore the significance of self-compassion and the role it plays in long-term stress management and anxiety relief.

Seeking Professional Help

Recognizing the Value of Professional Support

Foundation: While friends and family offer valuable support, sometimes seeking help from a trained professional is essential.

Key Point: Professionals bring expertise and objective perspectives to the journey of managing stress and anxiety.

Signs Professional Help May Be Beneficial

1. Persistent Symptoms

Example: If anxiety symptoms persist despite self-help efforts.

Indicator: Consistent feelings of overwhelm, panic, or a sense of losing control.

2. Impact on Daily Life

Indicator: Anxiety significantly affecting work, relationships, or daily functioning.

Recognition: When stress interferes with your ability to lead a fulfilling life.

The Role of Mental Health Professionals

1. Therapists and Counselors

Approaches: Cognitive-behavioral therapy (CBT), talk therapy, or other evidence-based modalities.

Objective: Addressing thought patterns and behaviors contributing to anxiety.

2. Psychiatrists

Expertise: Specialized in prescribing medications to address chemical imbalances.

Collaboration: Often works in conjunction with therapists for comprehensive care.

Overcoming Stigma

Reality Check: Seeking professional help is a proactive step toward well-being, not a sign of weakness.

Education: Encourage a shift in perspective by sharing the benefits of therapy.

Finding the Right Professional

1. Research and Referrals

Ask for Recommendations: Seek referrals from friends, family, or primary care providers.

Online Resources: Explore reputable therapist directories.

2. Initial Consultation

Objective: Use the first meeting to assess the therapist's approach and determine compatibility.

Tip: Don't hesitate to try multiple therapists to find the right fit.

Real-world Example

Case Study: Michael's Therapeutic Journey

Michael sought therapy to address workplace stress and found relief through cognitive-behavioral techniques.

Tip: Your therapeutic journey is unique—find a professional who aligns with your needs.

The Importance of Consistency

Regular Sessions: Consistency is key for therapeutic progress.

Collaboration: Work collaboratively with your therapist to set achievable goals.

Call-to-Action

1. Research Professionals: Begin the process of finding a mental health professional using reputable resources.
2. Initial Consultation: Schedule an initial meeting to discuss your concerns and assess compatibility.
3. Embrace the Process: Understand that therapy is a gradual process, and be open to the benefits it can bring.

Seeking professional help is a courageous step toward long-term relief from stress and anxiety. In the upcoming chapter, we'll explore the practice of self-compassion and its transformative role in the journey to well-being.

Chapter 7

Creating Your Anxiety-Free Zone

Designing Your Physical Space

The Impact of Environment on Well-being

Foundation: Your physical surroundings play a crucial role in influencing your mental and emotional state.
Key Insight: Purposefully crafting your living and working space can contribute to an anxiety-free zone.

Decluttering for Mental Clarity

1. Physical Clutter, Mental Clutter
Connection: A cluttered space can contribute to a cluttered mind.
Action: Systematically declutter your space, starting with one area at a time.

2. Simplifying the Environment

Guideline: Keep only items that serve a purpose or bring joy.

Effect: A simplified space promotes a sense of calm and order.

Creating Zones of Functionality

1. Work and Relaxation Zones

Separation: Clearly define spaces for work and relaxation.

Tip: Maintain boundaries to prevent work-related stress from permeating relaxation areas.

2. Personal Retreat Spaces

Example: Create a cozy reading nook or meditation corner.

Purpose: Provide a dedicated space for relaxation and self-care.

Natural Elements and Lighting

1. Bringing the Outdoors In

Benefits: Indoor plants and natural elements contribute to a calming atmosphere.

Consideration: Choose low-maintenance plants if you're new to gardening.

2. Optimal Lighting

Natural Light: Maximize exposure to natural light during the day.

Artificial Lighting: Use warm, soft lighting in the evening for a soothing ambiance.

Personalizing Your Space

Purpose: Surround yourself with items that hold positive associations and evoke a sense of comfort.

Example: Display photographs, artwork, or items that bring joy and connection.

Real-world Example

Case Study: Sarah's Tranquil Home Office

Sarah transformed her home office into a serene space with soft lighting, plants, and personal touches.

Tip: Tailor your space to reflect your preferences and create a sanctuary.

Mindful Technology Use

Technology Boundaries: Set designated times for technology use and create tech-free zones.

Purpose: Mitigate the stress associated with constant connectivity.

Call-to-Action

1. **Decluttering Session:** Dedicate time to decluttering a specific area in your living or working space.

2. **Create a Relaxation Nook:** Designate a small area for relaxation and personal retreat.

3. **Personal Touches:** Add personal items to your space that bring a sense of joy or connection.

Crafting your anxiety-free zone involves intentional choices in your physical environment. In the next chapter, we'll explore the practice of mindfulness and how it can be integrated into your daily life for lasting stress relief.

Implementing Daily Habits for Calmness

The Power of Daily Rituals

Foundation: Consistent daily habits can create a sense of routine and promote calmness.

Key Insight: Intentional practices contribute to a more mindful and centered way of living.

Morning Mindfulness Routine

1. Mindful Wake-Up

Approach: Avoid rushing out of bed; take a few moments to wake up mindfully.

Technique: Focus on your breath and set a positive intention for the day.

2. Mindful Breakfast

Practice: Eat breakfast without distractions, savoring each bite.

Effect: Sets a calm tone for the day ahead.

Mindful Breathing Throughout the Day

1. Mini Mindful Breaks

Integration: Pause for brief moments of mindful breathing throughout the day.

Benefit: Restores focus and reduce stress amid daily activities.

2. Cue-Based Breathing

Technique: Connect mindful breaths to specific cues, like receiving a message or stepping outside.

Outcome: Develop a habit of incorporating mindfulness into everyday moments.

Midday Reset

1. Mindful Movement Break

Activity: Engage in a short walk, stretch, or yoga session.

Result: Resets both body and mind, combating midday fatigue.

2. Gratitude Check-in

Practice: Take a moment to reflect on and express gratitude for aspects of your day.

Impact: Shifts focus from stressors to positive elements.

Evening Reflection and Unwind

1. Reflective Journaling

Exercise: Jot down thoughts and feelings from the day.
Purpose: Facilitates self-awareness and closure.

2. Technology Detox

Recommendation: Disconnect from screens at least an hour before bedtime.
Effect: Promotes relaxation and better sleep quality.

Real-world Example

Case Study: Alex's Mindful Workday

Alex incorporated short mindfulness breaks at work, reducing stress and improving focus.
Tip: Start with small, manageable changes in your daily routine.

Consistency is Key

Guideline: Implement one habit at a time and gradually build on your daily routine.
Reminder: Consistency enhances the effectiveness of mindful practices.

Call-to-Action

1. **Morning Intention Setting:** Begin tomorrow with a mindful wake-up and positive intention.
2. **Midday Mindful Break:** Pause for two minutes of mindful breathing during the busiest part of your day.
3. **Reflective Journaling:** Spend 10 minutes in the evening reflecting on the day's experiences.

Implementing daily habits for calmness is a transformative journey toward a more centered and mindful way of living. In the following chapter, we'll delve into the importance of self-compassion and how it can serve as a powerful tool in managing stress and anxiety.

Chapter 8

Overcoming Common Obstacles

Dealing with Relapses

Navigating the Ebb and Flow

Reality Check: The path to managing anxiety and stress is not linear, and setbacks are a natural part of the journey.

Key Insight: Understanding and addressing relapses is crucial for long-term progress.

Recognizing Relapse Signs

1. Resurfacing Symptoms

Indicator: Return of anxiety symptoms, such as heightened stress, intrusive thoughts, or disrupted sleep.

Recognition: Be attuned to changes in your emotional and physical well-being.

2. Behavioral Patterns

Signs: Reverting to previous coping mechanisms or habits.

Observation: Notice any shifts in behavior that may indicate a relapse.

Understanding Triggers

1. Identifying Triggers

Reflection: Explore potential triggers leading to the relapse.

Example: Work-related stress, life transitions, or external pressures.

2. Internal and External Factors

Internal: Reflect on personal thoughts, emotions, and self-talk.

External: Evaluate external factors contributing to stress.

Coping Strategies during Relapse

1. Revisit Coping Techniques

Return to Basics: Reengage with coping mechanisms that were effective in the past.

Techniques: Mindful breathing, journaling, or seeking support from your network.

2. Self-Compassion Practice

Mindset Shift: Treat yourself with kindness rather than self-criticism.

Mantra: "It's okay to face challenges, and I have the tools to overcome them."

Seeking Professional Support

1. Reconnect with Therapist or Counselor

Expert Guidance: Professionals can provide tailored strategies during challenging times.

Proactive Approach: Reach out before symptoms escalate.

2. Medication Adjustment Consultation

Psychiatric Support: If applicable, consult with a psychiatrist for potential adjustments.

Communication: Openly discuss any changes in symptoms or side effects.

Real-world Example

Case Study: Sarah's Relapse Resilience

Sarah faced a relapse but, with the support of her therapist, adjusted her coping strategies and emerged stronger.

Lesson: Relapses are opportunities for growth and refinement.

Developing a Relapse Prevention Plan

1. Reflective Analysis

Learn from the Experience: Identify triggers and coping gaps.

Preventive Measures: Develop strategies to address triggers proactively.

2. Regular Self-Check-ins

Routine Reflection: Periodically assess your mental and emotional well-being.

Adjustment: Modify coping strategies based on evolving needs.

Call-to-Action

1. **Self-Reflection:** Reflect on recent stressors and evaluate any signs of relapse.

2. Reach Out for Support: Contact a trusted friend, family member, or professional to discuss your experiences.

3. Update Coping Toolkit: Make adjustments to your coping strategies based on current needs.

Dealing with relapses is an integral part of the journey towards managing anxiety and stress. In the next chapter, we'll explore the transformative practice of self-compassion and how it serves as a cornerstone for emotional well-being.

Addressing Fear of the Future

Understanding the Fear

Common Experience: Fear of the future is a natural response to uncertainty.

Key Insight: Acknowledging and addressing these fears is vital for emotional well-being.

Identifying Specific Concerns

1. Personal Reflection
Questioning: What specific aspects of the future are causing anxiety?

Insight: Pinpointing concerns allows for targeted coping strategies.

2. Cognitive Exploration
Challenge Negative Thoughts: Examine and challenge irrational or catastrophic thinking about the future.

Reality Check: Assess the likelihood and severity of feared outcomes.

Embracing Mindfulness

1. Present-Moment Focus
Technique: Ground yourself in the present moment through mindful breathing or observation.

Purpose: Redirecting focus from the uncertain future to the tangible present.

2. Mindful Acceptance
Mindset Shift: Accepting that uncertainty is a part of life's journey.

Benefits: Reduces resistance to the unknown and fosters resilience.

Goal Setting and Action Plans

1. Concrete, Short-Term Goals
Define Achievable Steps: Break down long-term concerns into manageable short-term goals.

Example: Instead of focusing on a career change, set a goal to update your resume.

2. Action-Oriented Approach

Focus on What You Can Control: Direct energy toward aspects within your control.

Empowerment: Taking action fosters a sense of empowerment and reduces helplessness.

Building a Support System

1. Open Communication

Share Fears with Loved Ones: Discuss your concerns with friends or family.

Validation and Support: Often, voicing fears can lead to valuable insights and emotional support.

2. Professional Guidance

Therapeutic Support: Consult with a therapist for tools and coping strategies.

Objective Perspective: Professionals can provide guidance on managing future-related anxiety.

Real-world Example

Case Study: Jake's Journey to Empowerment
Jake addressed his fear of the future by setting small goals and seeking support from friends and a career counselor.
Lesson: Action and support are potent antidotes to the fear of the unknown.

Cultivating Flexibility

1. Adaptive Mindset
Flexibility: Embrace the idea that plans may change, and that's okay.

Adaptability: Cultivate a mindset that can adjust to unexpected turns.

2. Learning from Setbacks
Resilience Building: View challenges as opportunities for growth and learning.

Reflection: Extract lessons from setbacks and apply them to future endeavors.

Call-to-Action

1. **Fear Identification:** Reflect on specific fears related to the future.
2. **Goal Setting:** Define short-term, actionable goals to address those fears.
3. **Support Network Strengthening:** Reach out to a trusted friend or professional to discuss your concerns.

Addressing the fear of the future involves a combination of mindfulness, practical goal-setting, and building a strong support system. In the next chapter, we'll explore the transformative practice of self-compassion and its profound impact on managing anxiety and fostering emotional well-being.

Chapter 9

Mind-Body Connection

Holistic Approaches to Anxiety Management

Embracing the Unity of Mind and Body

Foundation: Recognizing the interdependence of mental and physical well-being is essential for comprehensive anxiety management.

Key Insight: Holistic approaches consider the integration of mind, body, and spirit for lasting well-being.

Mindful Movement Practices

1. Yoga for Mind-Body Harmony

Mindful Postures and Breathing: Combines physical postures with intentional breathwork.

Benefits: Promotes relaxation, flexibility, and mental focus.

2. Tai Chi for Flowing Energy

Slow, Controlled Movements: Blends meditation with gentle, flowing movements.

Effect: Enhances balance, reduces tension, and fosters mental clarity.

Breath-Centered Techniques

1. Diaphragmatic Breathing

Deep Belly Breaths: Engage the diaphragm for slow, intentional breathing.

Outcome: Activates the body's relaxation response, reducing anxiety.

2. Box Breathing Technique

Inhale, Hold, Exhale, Hold: Structured breathing pattern in a square shape.

Stress Reduction: Resets the nervous system and promotes a calm state.

Progressive Muscle Relaxation (PMR)

1. Systematic Muscle Tension and Release

Technique: Sequentially tense and then release muscle groups.

Purpose: Releases physical tension and encourages overall relaxation.

2. Body Scan Meditation

Mindful Awareness of the Body: Gradually focus attention on each part of the body.

Benefits: Promotes relaxation and cultivates mind-body connection.

Holistic Nutrition and Hydration

1. Balanced Nutrient Intake

Whole Foods Emphasis: Prioritize a diet rich in fruits, vegetables, lean proteins, and whole grains.

Impact: Supports both physical and mental health.

2. Hydration for Mental Clarity

Water's Cognitive Benefits: Staying hydrated aids in cognitive function and emotional balance.

Recommendation: Aim for daily water intake suitable for your body weight.

Real-world Example

Case Study: Maya's Mind-Body Transformation

Maya integrated yoga, diaphragmatic breathing, and mindful nutrition into her routine, experiencing a profound shift in anxiety levels.

Tip: Holistic practices are customizable; explore what resonates with you.

Integrative Approaches

1. Acupuncture and Acupressure
Traditional Chinese Medicine: Targets specific points to balance energy flow.
Research: Some studies suggest efficacy in reducing anxiety symptoms.

2. Meditative Practice
Mindfulness Meditation: Cultivates present-moment awareness.
Loving-Kindness Meditation: Focuses on compassion, fostering a positive mindset.

Cultivating Holistic Lifestyle Habits

1. Quality Sleep
Prioritization: Ensure sufficient and restful sleep.
Connection: Sleep profoundly impacts both mental and physical resilience.

2. Regular Physical Activity
Variety: Engage in a mix of aerobic exercise, strength training, and mindful movement.
Benefits: Enhances mood, reduces tension, and supports overall well-being.

Call-to-Action

1. Choose a Mindful Movement Practice: Explore yoga, tai chi, or another mindful exercise.
2. Incorporate a Breathing Technique: Start with diaphragmatic breathing for relaxation.
3. Mindful Nutrition: Integrate whole, nutrient-rich foods into your diet.

Holistic approaches to anxiety management provide a multifaceted toolkit for promoting well-being. In the final chapter, we'll delve into the transformative practice of self-compassion and its profound impact on the journey to emotional resilience and sustained calmness.

Integrating Spirituality and Mental Well-being

Understanding the Role of Spirituality

Holistic Perspective: Recognizing the interconnectedness of spirituality and mental well-being.

Key Insight: Integrating spiritual practices can provide profound support in the journey to emotional resilience.

Personal Exploration of Spirituality

1. Reflecting on Beliefs

Contemplation: Consider personal beliefs, values, and their role in your life.

Questioning: Explore how spirituality contributes to your sense of purpose and connection.

2. Mindful Presence in Spiritual Practices

Mindfulness in Prayer or Meditation: Engage in spiritual practices with present-moment awareness.

Outcome: Deepens the connection between the mind and the spiritual self.

Finding Meaning and Purpose

1. Connecting with Core Values

Identification: Identify and prioritize values that resonate with your authentic self.

Alignment: Aligning actions with core values fosters a sense of purpose.

2. Service and Contribution

Acts of Kindness: Engage in acts of service and kindness.

Effect: Cultivates a sense of fulfillment and interconnectedness.

Cultivating Gratitude

1. Gratitude Practices

Gratitude Journaling: Regularly reflect on and record moments of gratitude.

Shift in Perspective: Focusing on blessings enhances overall well-being.

2. Expressing Gratitude in Community

Share Your Appreciation: Communicate gratitude to friends, family, or community members.

Community Connection: Strengthens bonds and promotes a positive environment.

Mindful Meditation and Prayer

1. Mindful Meditation
Technique: Use mindfulness meditation to connect with your spiritual self.
Outcome: Enhances inner peace and mental clarity.

2. Personalized Prayer Practices
Individualized Approach: Tailor prayer practices to align with personal beliefs.
Source of Comfort: Prayer can provide solace during challenging times.

Real-world Example

Case Study: James' Spiritual Renewal
James explored mindfulness meditation and prayer, finding a profound sense of peace and purpose.
Tip: Personalize your spiritual practices to resonate with your unique beliefs.

Connecting with a Spiritual Community

1. Community Engagement

Joining a Spiritual Group: Participate in a community that shares similar beliefs.

Supportive Environment: Offers a sense of belonging and mutual support.

2. Spiritual Guidance

Mentorship or Counseling: Seek guidance from spiritual leaders or mentors.

Individual Support: Provides personalized insights and encouragement.

Embracing Acceptance and Surrender

1. Letting Go of Control

Surrendering to the Divine: Embracing the idea that certain aspects are beyond personal control.

Relinquishing Anxiety: Eases the burden of trying to control every outcome.

2. Acceptance Practices

Mindful Acceptance: Applying mindfulness to accept thoughts and emotions without judgment.

Inner Peace: Cultivates a serene acceptance of the present moment.

Call-to-Action

1. **Personal Reflection on Spirituality:** Consider your beliefs and how they contribute to your well-being.
2. **Incorporate Mindfulness into Spiritual Practices:** Apply present-moment awareness to prayer or meditation.
3. **Engage in a Spiritual Community:** Connect with others who share similar beliefs and values.

Integrating spirituality into mental well-being provides a holistic approach to emotional resilience. As we conclude this journey, the final chapter will explore the transformative power of self-compassion and its profound impact on sustained calmness and inner peace.

Chapter 10

Thriving Beyond Anxiety

Setting and Achieving Personal Goals

Embracing the Journey to Thriving

Culmination of the Journey: Setting and achieving personal goals is a pivotal step toward transcending anxiety and fostering lasting well-being.

Key Insight: The process of goal-setting provides direction, purpose, and a tangible roadmap for personal growth.

Reflection on Progress

1. Acknowledging Growth
Reflect on the Journey: Consider the progress made in managing anxiety.
Positive Reinforcement: Acknowledge achievements, both big and small.

2. Learning from Challenges

Resilience Building: Identify lessons learned from challenges.

Adaptive Strategies: Use insights to refine coping mechanisms and strategies.

Clarifying Values for Goal Alignment

1. Identification of Core Values

Core Values Exploration: Define personal values that align with your authentic self.

Guiding Principles: Values serve as a compass for goal-setting.

2. Alignment of Goals with Values

Purposeful Goals: Ensure that set goals resonate with core values.

Intrinsic Motivation: Goals linked to values provide deeper motivation.

SMART Goal Framework

1. Specific and Clear Goals

Clarity: Clearly define the goal to avoid ambiguity.

Example: Instead of "Reduce stress," specify "Incorporate daily mindfulness for stress reduction."

2. Measurable Progress

Tangible Metrics: Set criteria to track and measure progress.

Example: "Practice mindful breathing for 10 minutes daily."

3. Achievable Targets

Realistic Expectations: Ensure that goals are challenging yet attainable.

Example: "Gradually increase daily physical activity, aiming for 30 minutes."

4. Relevance to Values

Alignment with Values: Ensure that goals align with personal values.

Example: "Enhance social connections through regular, meaningful interactions."

5. Time-Bound Deadlines

Establish Timeframes: Set specific deadlines for goal completion.

Example: "Achieve a consistent sleep schedule within the next four weeks."

Breaking Down Goals into Actionable Steps

1. Incremental Progress

Step-by-Step Approach: Break down larger goals into manageable, actionable steps.

Example: "Research and enroll in a mindfulness class by the end of the month."

2. Building on Success

Progressive Goals: Use achieved goals as building blocks for subsequent objectives.

Example: "Expand mindfulness practice to include meditation after mastering mindful breathing."

Celebrating Achievements

1. Recognition of Milestones

Celebrate Small Wins: Acknowledge and celebrate each step forward.

Motivational Boost: Positive reinforcement enhances motivation.

2. Cultivating a Growth Mindset

Viewing Challenges as Opportunities: Embrace setbacks as opportunities for learning and growth.

Resilience: A growth mindset fosters resilience in the face of obstacles.

Real-world Example

Case Study: Emily's Goal Triumph
Emily set specific, values-aligned goals, such as incorporating daily gratitude practices and engaging in regular exercise.
Tip: Personalize your goals to align with your unique values and aspirations.

Integration of Self-Compassion

1. Kindness Amidst Challenges
Self-Compassionate Language: Practice self-compassion when facing setbacks.
Example: "It's okay to face challenges; I will learn and grow from this experience."

2. Adaptability in Goal Revision
Flexible Adjustments: Be open to revising goals based on evolving needs.
Example: "If a goal becomes unrealistic, I can adapt and modify it to better suit my current situation."

Call-to-Action

1. **Reflect on Achievements:** Acknowledge progress made in managing anxiety.
2. **Define Values:** Clarify personal values that will guide goal-setting.
3. **Create SMART Goals:** Develop specific, measurable, achievable, relevant, and time-bound goals.

Setting and achieving personal goals marks the culmination of the journey to thriving beyond anxiety. In the conclusion, we'll explore the transformative practice of self-compassion and its enduring impact on sustaining calmness and inner peace.

Embracing a Life Without Constant Stress

Reflecting on the Journey

Culmination of Efforts: Congratulations on reaching this point in your journey toward a life free from constant stress.

Key Insight: Reflect on the progress made, challenges overcome, and the commitment to well-being.

Embracing Self-Compassion

1. Foundational Practice

Unwavering Support: Self-compassion serves as a consistent ally in times of stress.

Mindset Shift: Embrace self-kindness, understanding, and acceptance.

2. Cultivating a Gentle Approach

Release from Perfectionism: Allow room for imperfections without self-judgment.

Positive Reinforcement: Celebrate the efforts made, not just the outcomes.

Sustaining Mindfulness in Daily Life

1. Continued Mindful Practices
Integration into Routine: Maintain mindfulness in daily activities.
Present-Moment Awareness: Be fully engaged in each moment, fostering a sense of calmness.

2. Adaptive Coping Strategies
Flexible Application: Adjust coping mechanisms based on evolving needs.
Resilience Building: The ability to adapt contributes to long-term stress management.

Nurturing a Supportive Environment

1. Connection with Loved Ones
Strengthening Bonds: Cultivate relationships that offer understanding and support.
Mutual Growth: Healthy connections contribute to emotional well-being.

2. Professional Guidance
Ongoing Therapeutic Support: Maintain a relationship with mental health professionals.

Preventive Measures: Proactively seek support during challenging times.

Embracing Joy and Fulfillment

1. Rediscovering Joyful Activities

Reconnect with Passions: Engage in activities that bring joy and fulfillment.

Balance: Strive for a harmonious blend of work, leisure, and self-care.

2. Setting Boundaries

Protecting Well-being: Establish clear boundaries to prevent overwhelming stress.

Empowerment: Saying no when necessary is a powerful act of self-care.

The Continued Journey

1. Lifelong Learning and Growth

Curiosity and Exploration: Continue learning about stress management and mental well-being.

Adopting New Strategies: Embrace evolving techniques for sustained calmness.

2. Adapting to Life's Changes

Resilience in Transition: Life brings changes; develop resilience to navigate transitions.

Continued Goal Setting: Set new goals aligned with your evolving values and aspirations.

Your Personalized Toolkit

1. Reflective Practices

Journaling: Continue documenting thoughts and feelings for self-awareness.

Gratitude Rituals: Cultivate a mindset of appreciation for the positive aspects of life.

2. Daily Mindfulness

Breathing Exercises: Integrate mindful breathing into daily routines.

Momentary Awareness: Find opportunities for brief moments of mindfulness throughout the day.

Conclusion

In the pages of "The Anxiety-Free Zone: A Step-by-Step Guide to Managing Anxiety and Stress for Good," you've embarked on a transformative journey toward lasting calmness and emotional well-being. Together, we've explored the intricate landscape of anxiety, delving into practical strategies and empowering insights to navigate its challenges.

As we conclude this guide, I invite you to reflect on the profound shifts within yourself. You've not only learned to unmask anxiety, recognize triggers, and understand the science of stress but have also cultivated a personalized toolkit of mindfulness, self-compassion, and holistic well-being practices.

The journey doesn't end here, it evolves. You stand at the threshold of a life free from constant stress, armed with the wisdom to set and achieve meaningful goals, the strength to navigate setbacks with resilience, and the grace to embrace self-compassion in every step.

"The Anxiety-Free Zone" is not merely a book; it's a companion on your ongoing journey to sustained calmness. As you turn the last page, remember that the practices within these chapters are not final destinations but stepping stones toward a life of fulfillment, joy, and profound well-being.

May the wisdom gained here continue to be a guiding light on your path, illuminating the way to an anxiety-free existence. Your commitment to this journey is commendable, and as you embrace the possibilities beyond stress, may you thrive in the boundless expanse of your own anxiety-free zone.

Congratulations on your resilience, your growth, and your commitment to a life of enduring calmness. May your days be filled with peace, and may you continue to thrive beyond anxiety.